Personal Accounts

BOOKS BY ROBERT PHILLIPS

POETRY
Inner Weather
The Pregnant Man
Running on Empty
Personal Accounts

FICTION
The Land of Lost Content

CRITICISM
The Confessional Poets
Denton Welch
William Goyen

EDITOR
Aspects of Alice
Moonstruck: An Anthology of Lunar Poetry
Last and Lost Poems of Delmore Schwartz
The Collected Stories of Noël Coward
Letters of Delmore Schwartz
The Stories of Denton Welch

Ontario Review Press Poetry Series

PERSONAL ACCOUNTS
New & Selected Poems 1966–1986

Robert Phillips

Ontario Review Press / Princeton

Copyright © 1966, 1978, 1981, 1986 by Robert Phillips.
All rights reserved.
Manufactured in the United States of America.
First printing.

Library of Congress Cataloging in Publication Data

Phillips, Robert S.
Personal accounts.

(Ontario Review Press poetry series)
I. Title. II. Series.
PS3566.H5P47   1986   811'.54   85-28350
ISBN 0-86538-050-3
ISBN 0-86538-051-1 (pbk.)

Distributed by Persea Books, Inc.
225 Lafayette St.
New York, NY 10012

For

ELIZABETH SPENCER

and for

WINN & LAWRENCE BEALL SMITH

AUTHOR'S NOTE

Over a third of this volume consists of poems written during the past five years which have not appeared in book form. The earlier poems are selected from my three previous collections, now out of print: *Inner Weather* (1966), *The Pregnant Man* (1978), and *Running on Empty* (1981). Some of these poems have been revised.

The new poems originally appeared in *Chelsea* ("Tree Sequence," "Wear," "The Caves of Childhood"), *Graham House Review* ("Adam Speaks," "The Announcing Man," "The Wounded Angel"), *The Hudson Review* ("Killing Snakes in Sussex County," "Queen Anne's Lace"), *Light Year '84* ("Heavenly Day for a Do"), *Lips* ("A Garden Sitter"), *Manhattan Poetry Review* ("Monks," "Coming Attractions"), *The Nation* ("Chicory"), *The New Yorker* ("Inside & Out"), *The Ontario Review* ("Promising," "A Local Artist," "Chambered Nautilus," "Le Papillon," "Diane Arbus' Collaborations"), *The Poetry Review* ("Letter from Nina"), *Shenandoah* ("Here & There," "In the Dumps," "In August," "The Well-Tempered Performer"), *Southern Quarterly Review* ("Postlude"), *Tar River Poetry* ("The New American Muse," "The Tough Man"), *Three Rivers Poetry Journal* ("Portrait of a Lady," "Old People"), *Voices* ("Sunflowers," "Dandelions").

Thanks is due my editor, Raymond J. Smith, and his wife, Joyce Carol Oates, for the idea for this book.

The poems are arranged not chronologically but by topic, since I continue to explore certain concerns—preoccupations—from book to book. This volume's basic unit is the progression not of the poem but of the chapter.

R.P.

CONTENTS

When I speak to you about myself, I am speaking to you about yourself. How is it you don't see that?

—Victor Hugo

I

Middle Age Nocturnes

Middle Age: A Nocturne

The silver tea service
assembles, stands at attention
when you walk by.
Like some lost regiment,
it wears tarnished coats.

The grand piano bares
yellowed teeth as you
give it the brushoff.
You no longer tickle its fancy.
The feeling is mutual.

The liquor cabinet chokes
on dusty bottles. You're forbidden.
In the wines, sediment
settles like sentiment,
like expectations.

You visit your children's rooms.
In their sleep they breathe
heavily. In their waking
they bear new adulthood
easily. They don't need you.

In her dreams your wife sheds
responsibilities like cellulite,
acquires a new habit.
A gaunt nun of the old order,
she bends to a mystical flame.

All the pictures have been
looked at, all the books read.
Your former black mistress,
the telephone, hangs around;
there's no one you want to call.

But early this morning,
in the upper field—
seven young deer
grazing in the rain!

The Land: A Love Letter

for Judith

This hill and the old house on it
are all we have. Two acres,
more or less—half crabby lawn,
half field we mow but twice a year.

Some trees we planted, most gifts
of the land. The pine by the kitchen?
Grown twice as fast as our son. The bald
elm lost the race with my hairline.

The mulberry—so lively with squirrels,
chipmunk chases, and birds—
fell like a tower in the hurricane.
My chain saw ate fruitwood for weeks.

And the juniper, the one that all but
obliterated the view? Men cut it
down to make way for the new well and water-
pump. That pump should pump pure

gold: we lay awake engineering
ways to get it paid for. But we'll never
leave this mortgaged hill: This land
is changing as we change, its face

erodes like ours—weather marks,
stretch marks, traumas of all sorts.
Last night a limb broke in the storm.
We still see it sketch the sky.

We've become where we have been.
This land is all we have, but this love
letter is no more ours than anyone's
who ever married the land.

5

Soft & Hard

The night they came to carry you away
it was your sacroiliac, not your mind.
Poleaxed on your bed of pain, unmovable,
you who never took aspirin cried out
then for novocaine, codeine, anything.
Two men had to lift you onto the stretcher
in only panties and bra. Black. Blessedly opaque.

Every light in the room glared, the outside
world inside at last. I saw how it looked
to strangers: dolls, magazines, stuffed bears,
real kittens underfoot, books books everywhere—
like the Collier brothers, whose Bronx home,
after they died, was stacked with every newspaper
they ever read. The ambulance took you,

I was left surrounded by the wreckage.
Once, younger, we ran through the park,
saw squirrels burying nuts under fallen leaves.
"I think they do that to soften, not save them,"
you said. "To make the hard shells edible."
Dear one, how hard we tried to soften all
our edges with things. And by going underground.

Autumn Crocuses

Basketing leaves during earth's
annual leaf-taking, we realize
with a start—something's missing.
The autumn crocuses that would spring

each October by these rocks,
no longer here! We never planted
them, but they implanted themselves
on us. Now, for their lack,

we are poorer. Purest orchid color,
they astonished amidst the season's
dwindling. Crocuses in autumn?
How perverse! To reverse the seasons!

Every year we bore a bunch
into the house with pride,
surprising guests who'd never seen
their likes. They thought them

foreign, remote, inaccessible—
like edelweiss. No vase, glass, or jar
ever contained them. Their soft white stems
always bent, jack-eared blossoms

lolled like heads of old folks
sleeping in rocking chairs.
I read once where their yellow pistils
are a saffron source. For us,

source of satisfaction. Now gone.
A woodchuck? Early frost?
My failure to care for bulbs?
They were the unaccountable

we thought we could count on.

The Unfalling

November fifteenth, and still no fall
of leaves. They cling tenaciously
to every branch and stem. Weeks ago
they turned color, now turncoat
and will not let go. Even last night's
Sturm und Drang left them unperturbed.

In the country the bushel baskets
are impatient, awaiting their legacies,
their windfalls. Wheelbarrows stand
unmoving. Each suburban garage and cellar
houses rakes and yard brooms which lean
upon one another, mourning next-of-kin.

The gutters at my roofline are amazed:
Each autumn they strangle on leaves—
yet last night's rain set them singing
clear and high, a castrati choir.
All the baseballs boys lost last summer
long to be blanketed down for winter.

Will the leaves never fall?
Will this be the fall that failed?

Adam Speaks

"Sometime next month, when winter performs
her disappearing act, when the slate

of sky is wiped clean with clouds,
we will walk for twenty minutes or so

through loamy woods, staring at the discarded
beer bottles. (Where do all the bottles

and cans come from? Hunters pursuing their youth
in the snow? Lovers with no place else to go?)

We will walk and talk about the retaining wall
we're not really likely to build in the front yard,

the tulips which soon will be preening,
blossoms each year more diminished—

I never dig the bulbs to let them rest;
rest is something in short supply.

We will walk the dapple and slant of common North
American woods, kicking waves of pine needles

as if we were still in the Black Forest,
Sauerland, Vienna Woods, under the lindens,

as if we were still in Eden, sharing
our acre with the innocent fruit."

Promising

An uncompleted soapbox racing car
abandoned years ago in a garage
itches to compete in this spring's derby.

A not-bad oil portrait of someone's dad
executed by someone's mom when young
just took a shellacking. It won't improve.

An aging actor, once an attendant lord,
no more, looks for change on sidewalks.
He can't find any. There's less to lose these days.

Two lovers grow tired of one another,
climb pointed rocks below Montauk lighthouse.
They wonder when and why the light went out.

Figures of the Past

"In your memory it is
always summertime,
sunlight bright but pastel.
We have soft edges.
Were you to touch us
(it is *you* we find touching),
we would be velvet, dust-
pussies, woodland moss.

"We have no substance.
We exist only in mind.
Our diet, an inheritance
of air. To imagination's movement
we dance the synapse shuffle:
First teacher, first date,
Great-grandfather, lost love—
forever old, forever young—
we are here. Waiting. Accounted for.

"Unwind, rewind, rerun us at will.
We are a past of your reconstruction,
figments, Ophelias to your Hamlet.
History is rewritten daily.
Even as you read this,
we are perceptibly fading.
You will become one of us."

Inside & Out

Upstairs a young man plays
the stereo. From the ceiling
he watches himself dance like a cock.
No one understands him.

Outside the rain scribbles down
into the suburban garden
once ablaze with poppies,
peonies, salvia, impatiens,

seven varieties of loneliness.
Now the plot thickens
with weeds and poison ivy.
The picket fence wants painting.

The young man wants money,
but will not paint or weed.
Before the empty fireplace
the cat bites off a mouse's head.

In the morning kitchen a lemon
slice of sunlight spills
across a woman kneading dough.
Whole wheat, health food—

there is no health in it
for the young man. The bread
she bakes is bitter to the tongue.
It tastes of acrimony.

Downstairs in the master bath
a man sings a song
from the fifties: *Where are you,
lucky star? Now and forever!*

He would shake down his life
like a thermometer. He dries
his body, thickened like a pudding.
He leaves the mirror steamed—

he's weary of looking at himself.
The house creaks, an ancient sloop
going nowhere. The basement
carries the cargo of their lives.

Outside in the two-car garage
an aluminum rowboat is suspended
like a rocket ready to blast.
It's hung around for years.

Long ago the boy begged his father
to set the two of them adrift.
But the man fears depths,
and could not save them if they overturned.

Here & There

There was that winter a freezing of fire
and in tumbled nights the enlightening
of a pair, side by side, who were not there.
Though they shared a common bed, one flew out
west to San Diego, the other dreamed
a plaid figure on a New Hampshire mare.
From habit they slept spoon-fashion: Yin, Yang.
A transcontinental cold divided.

Their future seemed all of Manhattan's sky-
line, blacked out. Their match could not brighten that.
When spring came, oozing its thaw and its thud,
together they alone walked flowered fields,
stealing a blossom here, a blossom there,
and seeing nothing living, anywhere.

In August

Slow as the rhetoric of Warren G. Harding,
summer staggers to its knees, stunned
as a poleaxed steer at slaughter.

Beside the highway, vegetable stands groan,
sweet corn, peaches lolling like Rubens' nudes,
tomatoes red as Red Cross plasma.

In the fields, scarecrows are empty-headed
uncles. Ponds shadow green as Canada
geese fly by. Sand congregates in swimsuit crotches.

Day lilies trumpet the garden's four corners,
black-eyed susans meet the day's eye,
loosestrife floods the marshes with fire.

Chipmunks assume the shape of pears,
snakes snooze and dream of shrews,
robins bob for worms like apples in a barrel.

Air-conditioners sigh, captive dolphins;
dust-pussies lie under country beds;
crickets, domesticated Vivaldis.

Night drops, a lady's chemise, not too clean.
Insects, both sexes, dive-bomb the porch light.
The planet like love slowly turns to ice.

Wear

for Philip Booth

Your car, just paid for, begins to rust.
Rocker panels hoard salt like housewives
in wartime, pit and corrode. Under the hood
bearings and rings, points and valves
collect dirt, do the old slow burn.

You barely recognize your own living room.
But the tired buttons on the tufted sofa
wink. They know you well. It's unsettling.
Whenever you enter, bare threads, tears,
plaster flakes rush up to embrace you.

The English settee, your pride, collapsed—
an athlete gone to pot. The Siamese cat
shredded your favorite reading chair.
Nothing has nine lives, or even two. The wine
stain on the carpet assumes your own silhouette.

Yet there's consolation. Damaged goods
don't worry about becoming damaged. Your women
prefer an older lover, or so they say.
There's a bald look, so go for it! Raccoons
grow fat on garbage. Poets recycle poems.

Monks

I think of the poverty of monks
and burn my last dollar. Drink
vinegar and clear my room bare
as a cell. One image remains:
you in your Jaguar, driving away,
the car crème and rich as marzipan.

I write to you, but it is not
a correspondence; you never answer.
When I write I think of how
you drank Perrier and lime
before *anyone* drank Perrier.
(On rare sprees, lime gimlets
from Rose's Lime Juice and gin—
"Anne Sexton's favorite!"
You grinned like a skull.)
Of you naked, yoga on a mat in moonlight,
breasts swaying like two baby seals.
Of you stepping out on Village streets,
purple stretch pants, green cape,
Puss in Boots. On our lovebed
your breath was fire, Saint Teresa
in her frenzy. I attempt to translate
Latin, Greek. To translate is to learn
one's own language. (What is mine?)
Monks are the richest men.
They make God their only god.

Cell of spirit,
contain me now.
Simple fare,
sustain me now.
I write this letter
in holy water.

For months I have not paid the phone bill.
Lift the receiver, speak to a dead ear.
I no longer subscribe to electricity.
At sundown I cannot see what I have tried
to say. At sundown you are braking
your Jaguar in your attached garage.
A monk has no attachments, they say.

Coming Attraction

It always appears more appealing
    than the film
you've come to see. Carefully edited

(unlike life), it promises promise,
    glamor, escape—
a new Grace Kelly you've never seen,

cool, unruffled, serene as she hangs
    by her capped teeth
from a helicopter blade. The feature

you paid four-fifty for? All talk,
    talk, talk. You explore
the seat beneath your seat—a wad

of old gum, perhaps something worse,
    stuck like a seal,
hardened, all juices dried (like life).

The popcorn which smelled of childhood
    is stale. This motion
picture you are watching, mere light

play upon a silvered screen. It is not
    going to make a motion
to change your ways, it is not going

to give focus to the brief surprise
    which is your life,
it is not going to slide beneath

cold cotton sheets. No matter how
    often you come back,
you go home more alone than before.

Chicory

I walk the roadsides and damp wasteplaces
looking for wildflowers. Soon I find
tall clumps of my favorite,
bluest of blue flowers, the chicory,
growing close along stiff-branched stems.
No leaves to speak of, blue says it all.
I pick a dozen and carry them home
like a prize. Placed in an antique
cut-glass vase, they are my possession.
In an hour the bright blue petals close
like the sight of the old,
or something killed on the road.
So it has been with us, my dear,
having each been plucked from its element.

Sunflowers

How bold, how vivid the sunburst of your bloom.
    Yellow rays, you proclaim the summer
with more exuberance and broom stamina
        than all croaking frogs of the season.
You blazon forth your feverish glow,
        brave blond flames meet and match August,
heat for heat. And how brilliantly you defy
        autumn: blossoms curl like smoke puffs,
kindled bronze, aglow like rust-dapplings,
        molten orange stains. You stand, backbones
stiffening in the breeze, stalking your ground—
        phoenix of flowers, pillar of fire—
then in umber silence, you burn yourselves out.

Dandelions

Tiny heads popping up, yellow as butter,
    they encroach upon the world's front yard
and gather in gregarious lawn parties
    which seem to arrest the season.

Towheads together bobbing gaily,
    frail effulgence of hyacinthine curls,
their life is a summer of festivals.
    They think that they will live forever.

Yet soon enough light heads are gray,
    in the first thin wind they scatter.
Year after year they teach us
    how soon we disappear.

Decks

In the fair fields of suburban
counties there are many decks—
   redwood hacked from hearts
   of California giants, cantilevered
   over rolling waves of green
   land, firm decks which do not
   emulate ships which lean and list,
   those wide indentured boards which
   travel far, visit exotic ports of call.
   No. Modern widows' walks,

these stable decks, stacked with foldup
chairs, charcoal bags, rotogrills,
   are encumbered as the Titanic's.
   They echo Ahab pacing the Pequod,
   the boy who stood on the burning,
   Crane's jump into the heart of ice,
   Noah craning for a sign, a leaf . . .
   These decks are anchored to ports
   and sherries which mortgaged house-
   wives sip, scanning horizons,

ears cocked for that thrilling sound,
the big boats roaring home—
   Riviera, Continental, Thunderbird!
   Oh, one day let these sad ladies
   loose moorings, lift anchor, cast
   away from cinderblock foundations.
   Let the houses sail down Saw Mill,
   Merritt, Interstate. You will see
   them by the hundreds, flying flags
   with family crests, boats afloat

only on hope. Wives tilt forward, figureheads.
Children, motley crew, swab the decks.

       Let the fleet pass down Grand Concourse,
       makes waves on Bruckner Boulevard.
       Wives acknowledge crowds, lift pets.
       The armada enters Broadway, continues
       down to Wall. Docked, the pilgrims
       search for their captains of industry.
       When they come, receive them. They harbor
       no hostilities. Some have great gifts.

In the Dumps

for Howard Moss

On the back seat, six plastic bags,
securely tied, that stink the morning air:
Driving through the woods to Fireplace Road,
the world is too much with you, as you think.

Such places are a smoking zoo, mostly rats;
this one, East Hampton's dump, is orderly:
fair-copy manuscript of a fugue by Bach,
a Swiss sanitation engineer's ideal.

Ringed by bayberry acres, one rough alp
consists of bottles, another is tin cans;
that flatbed is newspapers fastidiously stacked.
Beyond, the raw ravine engorges all,

an ungrand canyon. There are no outcast
Frigidaires, truck tires, bedsprings—usual
oddments of uselessness. "Take a dump"
no longer means "to void." Waste is compacted,

renamed, recycled, rising to new life—
Lazarus among the rinds and coffee grounds!
You stare into the heap, in love with its ripe
backside. The twenty-first century is here.

Greedy gulls inscribe the salty air,
cruising their next feed. To them this crap
appears a quilt, patchwork-colorful
(if birds see colors, which you rather doubt).

In Bangladesh—this could be Bangladesh!—
such rotten landfill would be a windfall
to those who never even entered the ratrace.
Beauty is in the eye of the beholden.

A man with his dog strolls by, they disappear
as you sort, stack, fold, heave: Loneliness
collapses inward like a beer can crushed
in your hand. Night sweats and low finance.

Sort, stack, fold, heave. All flesh is grass,
not plastic which will see this planet out.
Now as your leave you take permanent leave,
consumer consummately consumed at last.

II

Ninety Miles from Nowhere

Vertical & Horizontal

Mother grew up in the Blue Ridge,
thriving on the various landscape,
Southern sounds, the thin air.
He married her, brought her heirlooms,
antiques, pretensions back to Delaware,
back to the only town he ever knew
or felt comfortable in. Mother fell
in love with a uniform, not knowing
how uniform life could be.

Ensconced, immediately she felt oppressed
as teacher's wife, and by the heavy air.
(Could a soufflé ever rise in it?)
"It's not so much the heat," she remarked,
"it's the humility." The landscape?
Unrelentingly flat—not one hill
within ninety miles. The natives'
accent? Flat. The townspeople? Flat
-footed. Even the songbirds songed off-key.

Father never noticed—he,
whose favorite catch was flounder.
Every morning for decades she rose,
deflated, a vertical soul snared
within an horizontal landscape,
knowing a steamroller had run over her life.
And once a year Mother returned
to Virginia, head lifted high, and pretended
she never had come down in this world.

The Mole

"There goes the Mole!" Mother cried.
"You children look quick or you'll miss
him!" It was Father, disappearing down
the cellar stairs. Every day he'd retreat
to his radio shack, stay past midnight.

He'd built a rig others envied, came
from miles around to see. Every day
he'd jam the airwaves, ruin the block's TV.
Every day we'd hear him sit before the mike
calling "CQ, CQ calling CQ" to whoever
listened at the other end. He once
claimed to reach Moscow. "Ralph's the handle,
calling from W2CAT, the Old Cat Station—
W-2-CAT-Alley-Tail." He *was* a handsome cat;
Mother once adored him, I know.

But what I'll never know is, Why he'd talk
to any stranger far away and not once
climb back up the stairs to the five of us
to say, "Hello . . . hello . . . hello . . . hello."

Once

"Mother, what is Labor Day?" I once
asked. "That, my dear, is when everybody

else in the country goes to the beach
except us," she said over her heavy iron,

her heavy irony. Why everybody else,
not us? Was there a national lottery?

Had our family, like blind Pew, drawn
the black spot? If not this year, could we

go the next? It was years before I understood.
One year we went to the beach. A new world,

half an hour away. I never had seen
the ocean. My big toe in the Atlantic!

Mother and the four of us on the beach,
Father on the boardwalk on a bench,

under an umbrella, wearing a ratty straw hat.
Suddenly he was somebody's old aunt!

(Once he'd gotten sun poisoning fishing,
he claimed.) He looked at his wristwatch a lot.

Mother wore an ancient wool bathing suit,
her legs thin as the stork's.

I leapt repeatedly into the muscled sea,
the sea rumpled, my brothers romped,

the sun felt good, the salt smelt good,
Jesus! it was fun, and we never went back.

31

The Whip

I will hire a master builder
to reconstruct my childhood
home. There will, first of all,
be a well-painted white bathroom

door directly opposite a tan
cellar door. That is essential.
On the inside of the bathroom door
the builder must screw a fat brass

hook and hang there a thick
braided horsewhip. Every time
I opened the bathroom door,
it swayed gently, like doom:

leather, heavy, a stinger
at the tip. That whip was the end
of all fear and fear of punishment
whenever Father flew up the cellar

stairs, raging—whenever childhood
brawls disturbed his solitude.
Father yanked down our pants, flailed
the air. Mother went and hid somewhere.

Once he broke it on my brother,
went to Sharptown, bought another.
Today I had drinks with Father.
We exchanged old jokes, pleasantries;

yet underfoot I heard feet pounding
up the stairs. Overhead,
that flicked lightning in the air.

Magic

My magic apparatus, my bag of tricks,
rests in the basement now. Cotton-batting rabbit,
mystical linking rings, multiplying billiard balls,
vanishing silk handkerchiefs, feather bouquets—
the preoccupations of a childhood spirited away—
beckon, Svengali-fashion, still.
The lure of chicanery remains.

Stored there, those pretty deceptions,
those fabulous feats of legerdemain,
should seem tawdry to me now.
All lacquer, gilt and glitter cannot conceal
the illusion of illusions. Only children deceive
and are themselves deceived.
The adult mind discovers the trick.

Any day was a good day to practice my magic.
A corner of the attic was reserved
for the black table, its embroidered silver moons
ordered from some Philadelphia prestidigitator.
I was a moon-gazer night and day!
Hours then disappeared for a boy
behind a necromantic table:

It didn't matter if the boy could not hit
a home run, perfect a flying tackle.
Every day had a false bottom.
The mawking outside could not reach
that enchanted tower with its conjurer.
But magician, charmer, pale wizard,
you practiced your tricks too well:

Sleight of hand must be outgrown.
Mere magic cannot stay the mind.
The boy becomes a man of shopworn tricks,
in a world with no trapdoor.

Flatworms

In biology class we decapitated them,
truncating their bodies, too.
We boys had fun; girls cringed or gagged.

Yet within a week, each half gave rise
to a new half, and head as good as new.
Miracle enough the worms survived.

More miracle, their recapitulation.
I named mine John the Baptist, Anne Boleyn,
Sir Thomas More, and Mary Queen of Scots,

and marvelled that such wriggling things
accomplished what queens and martyrs could not.

Views of the Astrologers

Ancient and fabulous, they ride across
the jacket, *The Wonder Book of Bible
Stories* (the one I loved best as a boy,
two hundred fifty-two pages, sixty
illustrations by unnamed "E. P. J.");

mounted on camels, led by lank black boys,
they traverse west, faces stained by the grape
night. One raises a finger, gnarled vine.
Overhead that star, too magnificent
to illustrate, glows only in the mind's

imagination, and in rich glintings
off the camel robes' swaying lamé fringe.
The camels smirk smugly, as camels do,
long-lashed eyes sealed in secret camel-thoughts.
No weariness, no suffering, no sweat.

These for me will always be The Wise Men.
Sassetta's Sienese tempera on wood,
albeit a masterpiece, is a fake:
three kings on three horses black, brown and white,
one king wearing a hat of Persian lamb!

And who are those unlikely hangers-on,
two striplings and one tricorn Bonaparte?
Give me my camels and my lonely three
(from Persia, India, Ethiopia?):
King Caspar, King Melchior, King Balthazar.

How did we even come to know their names?
Only Saint Matthew paid them lip service,
Luke atwitter over shepherds, Saints Mark and John
not one word. But "E. P. J." portrayed them
truly: *Wonder Book*, Nineteen Twenty-two.

Scissors Grinder

He
set spring
into motion each year
with his
wheel

No
storms came
down or screens went
up before his
fire

-works
children ran
to see sparks dance (in
-candescent angels
on pins)

For
nickels and dimes
his rotary righted every
hoe axe mower
marriage

Till
stainless
steel made in Japan
orphaned the ancient
cutlery

Then
no scissors etc.
just children come to love
the wheel with empty
hands

He
went. Never
came back this spring or last.
The seasons cleave to one
another,

don't
change, and
all the just-new knives
are dull, they blunt
the days:

Life,
that old
case of knives,
has lost its
edge.

Killing Snakes in Sussex County

There was no amnesty
for snakes. Whenever
we saw one on our property,
we ran and got the hoe,
Father chopped off its head.
Mostly harmless water snakes,
but a snake was loathed.
How the headless bodies
writhed! Muscles undulated
till sundown. We were careful
where we walked; every snake
in the grass has a mate.
Once Mother reached into
the hedge for the hose,
extricated a black snake
instead. Once I lazed
on a dock, legs dangling
in the water. A fat one
ascended my shin like
a patient lover. And
once Father encountered
a copperhead—poisonous!—
dozing on our doormat.
Our campaign vindicated,
Father's picture appeared
in the paper, the longest
copperhead on record twined
on his hoe. Father grins,
snake's mouth's one long grin.

When the blade strikes,
the snake leaves the snake.
Like shedding a skin.
Slow roil of scale
and pointed tail, coil
of steel, true vine

of nesting turmoil,
tongue of lightning forked,
low energy, cold blood—
the trail left in the dust
by its body is an engraver's
mark, a hollow for holy water,
clean as a snake's mouth.
The snake with its attendant
serpentines dreams of royal
dispensation. A snake
full of delight slides
toward a hoe of death.

Running on Empty

As a teenager I would drive Father's
Chevrolet cross-county, given me

reluctantly: "Always keep the tank
half full, boy, half full, ya hear?"—

the fuel gauge dipping, dipping
toward Empty, hitting Empty, then

—thrillingly!—way below Empty,
myself driving cross-county

mile after mile, faster and faster,
all night long, this crazy kid driving

the earth's rolling surface
against all laws, defying physics,

rules and time, riding on nothing
but fumes, pushing luck harder

than anyone pushed before, the wind
screaming past like the Furies . . .

I stranded myself only once, a white
night with no gas station open, ninety miles

from nowhere. Panicked for a while,
at standstill, myself stalled.

At dawn the car and I both refilled.
But Father, I am running on Empty still.

Portrait of a Lady

Color snapshot, circa 1960.

Red velvet Victorian, the chair she sits on like a throne
belonged to her father's family, who also once possessed
"the finest horse-drawn carriage in all of Christiansburg!"
(The matching loveseat, on which her husband could not sprawl,
was presented to a son and quixotic daughter-in-law,
who replaced red velvet with cheap yellow cotton corduroy.
She could have cried at such desecration, but did not.)

Over her shoulder, two outsize stereo speakers (Danish
modern, rectangular) tower anachronistically
to the feminine form of the ancestral chair. They are
elephants trampling a daisy field. They surfeit the green
and rose room with dance band, marching band, Dixieland.
She turns a deaf ear. Music and radio are not her cup of tea.
She has "The Girls" in to converse, play a little Bridge.

Over her head, hung too high, proportioned too small
for the wall, a framed reproduction of a painting,
"Dogwood in a Vase." It is one of a matched pair,
a Mother's Day gift once, before the children moved away
and left her there. On one chair arm she curls a hand
like Mona Lisa. The other rests in her lap modestly,
displaying her genuine diamond-chip engagement ring.

This was the beginning of her life's matinee,
before the Cadillac she wanted but was too sick to use,
before aristocratic fingers curled with arthritis,
before hair lightninged gray, the future cupped within
like a wooden Russian doll which, opened, reveals inside
diminishing versions of herself. Here the smile is set,
the eyes defiantly gay. *I am still here*, is what they say.

The Announcing Man

Up in the tower of that Bingo stand,
installing amplifier and microphone,
my father wired the carnival for sound.

August sweat rivered his brow.
He crawled the octagonal structure,
screwed a speaker at every other corner.

Hornets, bees and webs plagued his head.
I was there to help—pass up tools,
hold a washer, do what a small boy can.

Equipment in place, he'd mount the stool,
test the mike: "One, two, three, four—
testing. This is a test. One, two, three,

four," then drop a 78 on the turntable,
throw the switch. The brassy blare
of John Philip Sousa skirled the air.

Then all Sharptown knew it was time,
the annual Firemen's Carnival commences!
Strings of colored lights magicked the sky.

At night my father returned, installed
himself in that tower, to call
till midnight countless Bingo games:

"N-29. G-7. B-13. Bingo? Do I hear
Bingo? Don't destroy your cards, folks,
let's check the winning card. That you,

Cooney? Good to see you! Call 'em out,
loud and clear." There was a merry-go-round,
a Ferris wheel, two raffled Chevrolets

and a freaky sideshow. But the center
of it all was Bingo, the center of *that*,
my Dad. For decades he called the game

that sent happy men and ladies home
clutching satin pillows, Navaho blankets,
fringy boudoir lamps, Kewpie dolls.

Every August the men who ran the stand
gave him pick of the litter.
He furnished our home with Bingo prizes.

Envoy:
Every August I miss that carnival
and its announcing man. This typewriter
is my microphone. I amplify as I can.

III
Brief Lives

Child of the Night

William Cullen Bryant, 1794-1878

"Bard of the river and of the wood,"
Whitman called you, "ever conveying
a taste of open air." Oh? Then why
do I sniff the claustrophobic tomb
whenever I revisit your poems?

Broken gleams never quite warmed
that cold dark air. Human voices
segued into imperial and lost elegies.
Autumn? Just so many dead flowers.
The present day? The year's saddest.

To write "Thanatopsis" at seventeen!
The preoccupation died hard. Late
in life it pursued you still; this time
you called it "The Flood of Years."
Was it the flood of early morning dips?

Fragile child, your head was said to be
pumpkin-large. Your physician father
shrunk it to normal. Each morning he dipped
you, headfirst, into an icy spring.
The water was dark and deep . . .

Small wonder James Russell Lowell
portrayed you as cool—"a smooth
silent iceberg that is never ignified."
Cullen, before Dickinson, Frost, Robert Lowell,
you were well acquainted with the night.

Le Papillon

Emma-Marie Livry, 1842-1863

Illegitimate daughter of a stage-
door-johnny and a sixteen-year-old danseuse,

Emma-Marie Livry was reared backstage
of the Paris Opéra, danced onstage

in her teens. Old Madame Taglioni observed,
"I must have danced rather like that,"

and commenced to choreograph her sole
ballet for young Livry, *Le Papillon*:

The heroine, transmogrified into
a magic butterfly, darts toward a torch

until the flame shrivels her fragile wings.
Make-believe. Yet in dress rehearsal

for a later, greater triumph, Emma brushed
her long diaphanous skirts against naked

gaslamps while waiting cue. Across the stage
she flew, carried on incandescent wings.

(She'd refused to dip her gauzy tutu
into fireproofing: "It makes it *dingy*!")

On she whirled about the stage, enveloped
in flame. She blazed, the element consumed.

Her spirit flickered for eight months
before she let go. Thus expired the apogee

of French romantic ballet; no danseuse
of comparable gifts waited in the wings.

At her funeral, Gautier testified,
over her bier a white butterfly danced!

Postlude

Conrad Aiken, 1889-1973

A rock in the crimson wind!
Your face turned toward
a three-fold kingdom:
England, New England,
the New South ambient.

You thronged the brief world.
The maelstrom had all of you.
From the wild verge of Cape
Cod rocks to Savannah swamps,
you shuffled, a deck of cards,

to turn face up in New York,
face down on the Sussex Coast.
Fleeing what? Death's caucus?
(Father killing Mother, himself?
The world bronzed. You were ten.)

Desolate, melancholy, unappeased,
your music's suspended cadences
crouched behind one wall or other,
stopped one clock or another.
You regretted public appearances,

unlike your fêted classmates
Eliot, Broun, Benchley, Lippman
(Harvard, '11). Aiken,
in the Rollie McKenna portrait
you peer, a spiritual Friar Tuck:

At nose's bridge your wen
becomes a third eye:
Cyclops, Shiva, Wadza
of Egyptian hieroglyphics—
divine. At the least, superhuman.

Watery suns, your blue-gray eyes.
Silver bullets, your martinis
consumed icy from antique silver
tennis trophies: energy and art,
libido and libation, linked at last.

Chambered Nautilus

Robert T. S. Lowell, 1917-1977

Just as the chambered nautilus, twenty-
    one rooms already accumulated,
        sensing the level of salient fluid
            fallen too low in its last-built chamber,
                begins to secrete a new partition,

You too sought preservation in new quarters
    whenever a crisis culminated.
        You'd take on yet another apartment,
            a new woman—one dancer, several poets—
                leaving wife and daughter chambered at home.

Oh nautilus shellfish, navy man's son,
    who fathoms such egressive behavior?
        In your going out was your coming in.
            Your works are disclosures of inclosures.
            Symmetry's your protection in retreat.

"A Local Artist"

Henry M. Progar, 1927-1982

Ex-flyboy, you came to us from Pennsylvania
hills, Penn's woods, and found beauty
in the flat farms, swamps, ponds, estuaries
of Delaware. While I was trying to get out,
you dug boot heels in. Your paintings revealed
the riches of abandoned barns, listing wharfs,
the wealth of earth tones: browns, grays, tans.

But I had to have the whole rainbow.
I split that flat scene while you painted it.
Today you are dead at fifty-five, too good
to be called "a local artist" whenever reviewed.
What is a local artist but an artist
who happens to live locally? What has art
to do with geography? Yet your oils

have everything to do with geography.
They view newly the local venue. Hank,
your landscapes are your nimbus, they
and your modest self-portrait—a young boxer
with broken nose in a white tee shirt,
contemplating, as deeply as Aristotle
the bust of Homer, a bird posed upon a stick.

Queen Anne's Lace

Isabella Gardner, 1915-1981

I came to the end of Long Island to gather
thoughts and conclude
some piece of writing or other.
Instead I found this mood:

grief over your sudden departure,
debris of our friendship's growth.
Belle, hours before your death
you called and we spoke. Later

I cried. You'd thanked me for what
I'd not remembered doing. Your purpose,
valedictory. You knew. That night
at the hotel, death gave room service.

Once I dedicated a poem to you
(you never saw it) on autumn crocuses.
Something in their rarity, I suppose,
reminded me of you:

After our one real quarrel, I struck
the dedication. It shames me now,
watching the rain, realizing
your gift was to bestow.

When I came to this Spartan place,
I couldn't take the bleakness,
so picked some Queen Anne's Lace
that choked the gravelled ways.

Jarred, it stayed rigorously vital,
and for weeks it reminded me of you—
not autumn, but a summer view—
delicate, indestructible.

Before we really met, I thought:
"Our American Edith Sitwell!"—commanding
in your sweeping cape of night,
imperiously tall, spangly earringed.

Like Dame Edith's, yours too was facade:
Inside, sitting dutifully in the music room
of a parents' Boston home, a little redhead
waited for someone to share a game.

A constellation of blossoms, each individually
stemmed, the blooms *are* lace, naturally,
but also fireworks, diamond clusters,
celestial spiders, snowflakes. So much

intricacy and simplicity! Your love
poems, Belle, one feels approach
their art. Inevitable spontaneity.
Just as these appear not merely white,

but an essence of white and green,
absence and presence, dying and living,
nothing in nature is sure. Like life.
Like Piaf, you had no regrets.

Queen Anne's Lace has no smell.
I remember yours—what was the perfume?
Always the same, feminine, eternal.
I'd know it in any room.

Hidden at the heart of the umbel,
one spot of black, like yours
acquaintances steered clear of,
toward the end. Drink uncovered it.

If removed, placed on white paper,
that dot is perceived as purple.

A touch of the royal?
A *trompe l'oeil*?

I remember best our evenings, a spot
called "Simply Good," where the cuisine
matched the name, and the talk—a riot
of anyone we'd ever known.

We brought wine, the owner had
no license. Taking license,
I told "naughty" jokes. You winced,
then laughed fully. Generous as a weed.

You dazzled, and only the odd friend
knew of the son, lost
somewhere in South America; lost,
too, the daughter in Bedlam; the husband

who kicked you out and married
a younger, only to summon you again,
a lifetime later, on his famous deathbed.
How you agonized that decision—

To go or not to go? You left well enough
alone. Belle, my coconspirator,
you survived, bereft,
haunting the Chelsea as before.

The Well-Tempered Performer

Glenn Gould, 1932-1982

*The purpose of art is not the release of a
momentary ejection of adrenaline but is,
rather, the gradual lifelong construction
of a state of wonder and serenity.*
—G. G.

1. Syracuse. The Early Sixties

When the Byronic wonder slouched onstage
he ignored his audience and worried
the knobs of his travelling piano bench.
Delicately he twisted left and right.
We thought it'd never strike its proper height.
We waited. It was August, the hall hot.
He wore a dark wool coat, sweater and scarf;
on his fingers were dark fingerless gloves.

When finally he began to perform,
his eyes just cleared the keyboard! How bizarre,
like his singing of the melodic strain,
which quite rivaled the piano.
(One critic: "Mr. Gould was in fine voice.")
But it was as if we'd never heard Bach,
the rhythms incisive as icicles,
the thickets of counterpoint clarified.

Afterward, in the moist receiving line,
he refused to shake anybody's hand
until he encountered Louis Krasner,
resigned now to conducting the local
symphony. "An honor," Gould said, offering
his hand as if it were Lalique: "I have
your recording of the Berg." "Ah, the Berg!
I *commissioned* it." The old man became younger.

57

2. Toronto. The Early Eighties

Past a pricey gift shop and discotheque,
in a shuttered prison-like studio,
Gould holed up in a touristy hotel.
Unshaven, paunchy, he greeted bellboys
formally when they delivered his tea.
He slept by day, wrote by night, and ordered
one expensive vegetarian meal
each dawn. Then proceeded to make phone calls.

Phone bills mounted monthly to four figures.
"I live on long distance!" he cried, stopping
to pop a Valium. It distanced him.
His concertizing career was annulled.
He conducted instead a long affair
with the tape machine. He'd tape, retape, dub,
redub, until the work was purified.
On occasion he escaped Toronto,

cruising the Carolina coasts sleekly
by dark Lincoln Continental with phone.
Once he sang Mahler to the polar bears
at the Toronto Zoo; they understood.
"These are the happiest days of my life!"
Stickler for structure, he rerecorded
his coup, *The Goldberg,* exactly twenty
years later. Then his demanding life erased.

IV

A Modern Gallery

Picasso's "Boy Leading a Horse"

It is a naked horse and a naked boy
    who have nothing at all in their nakedness
except loneliness shared, and dim destiny.

No one knows whether the horse mourns the evening,
or if the boy's mourning somehow touches the horse.

When they draw near they are always withdrawn,
    aloof from that evening to which they belong
(in the gray plane that encloses them).

If from one or the other comes suddenly
clarion call or lamentation, we should know

it is because it is evening for both of them—
    The boy's evening comes with the first shining star,
the horse's with the sight of hay.

Just two in time, more lonely with the dusk.

John Wilde's "Happy, Crazy American Animals and a Man and Lady at My Place"

A portly possum dangles by his tail
from my living-room rafter. He adroitly assails
reality from topside, where inquiring crows nest.
The fox in stony stance upon my chest
of drawers looks stuffed, but his bark of love
is such stuff as dreams are made of.

Brilliant-hued birds and somber bats
fly overhead. Underfoot a domiciled wildcat
bats a ball across my planks, beneath my eaves,
but those furry forepaws' claws are sheathed.
The panoplied armadillo has seized
upon shards of a vase which once I prized—

Oh, the vanity of earthly possessions!
The vase was broken in the animals' procession
that toppled my turvy vanity upon its side.
Which is real? The fox and armadillo, or I?
I think there's a leopard behind that door.
The back door is open still. Are there *more*?

A polar bear lurches to embrace me like a brother.
Wild ducks fly in one window and out the other,
following an inner weather I cannot know.
My house is modest. The plaster falls like snow.
It was my sanctuary, legacy for kin.
What kinship with these beasts, clambering in?

Antediluvian arteries pulse in time and quick
with those of a naked lady, prime and pink,
now prancing in step with the great hornéd stag;
the beat of their marching does not lag,
parading princely across cracked linoleum.
Something in her high society succumbs.

All out-of-doors wants in, all in-of-doors, out.
Something wild in the mildest of us shouts.
These creatures, sniffing in strange civility,
would huddle close and comfort us, if they could.

Giacometti's Race

Bone-stack
beanstalk
broomstick
clothespole
gangleshanks;
they are
the thin
man inside
every fat one
who clamors
to climb out.
Every jaw
a lantern,
every face
a lean,
hungry look.
Ancient
violence.
Violent
freshness.
Do not
trust them.
Do not
trust them.
But:
the beauty!
Tapers flicker
in vertical
air! Delicacy
of a hair!
Herring-gut
economy.
Studies
of the minimal.
Learn to
love them.

Water,
not milk.
Rail against
fear of paper
shadows. Teach
survival on
slender means.
Live off
the thin
of the land.

Charles Burchfield's World

for John I. H. Baur

In the late great paintings of Burchfield,
    all nature goes round and around!
        Cornstalks jig, crickets genuflect,
            clouds flap like cawing of crows. Those
        wild Burchfieldian nights! The wind
    is a fleet of shrouds. Disaster
explodes from church-bells' claps, tele-

graph wires all shrill. Lie still, lie still
    and think about fear of the dark,
        the mystery that lurks in the hearts
            of trees, in the guts of all stumps
        in still waters. Why is the air
    so heavy with flowers tonight?
Why the cicada's nerve-music?

The night's alive with idiot eyes
    of houses, a thousand wet houses
        that rot. Look: Frequent the alleys
            the same as boulevards. God is
        what you find under a rock, God
    is the face of a hollyhock
in the late great paintings of Burchfield.

66

Morris Graves' "Joyous Young Pine"

Silently, and all alone, with no one
    to witness before the moon's fine scrim,
the pine in jubilation lifts its limbs.

It is an exultant young priest, praying.
    In spirit it is a Zen master, praying.
The moon, its halo of immateriality.

Such strange textures, strange rhythms!
    White threads of moonlight, white writing
in the sky! Joy of the human heart.

Here wind soughs in greeny boughs.
    Here dew seeps through dry earth.
Here insects creep up limbs, while

this mere stripling of a tree dances—
    David before the Ark—invoking legends,
holy delights, mysteries.

Amy Jones' "A Bouquet for Judy"

Someone placed this bouquet upon the waters.
    Casual flowers meant to cheer. Childhood colors:
pink, yellow, green, blue. Loveable, touching. A starfall.

It is a bridal bouquet tossed away in ecstasy.
    It is a floral tribute never delivered to a talent.
It exists upon a plane beyond ecstasy and talent.

See how it is wrapped in newspaper, floating.
    See how it has nothing to do with news, floating.
See how it is neither above or below, real or unreal.

Surely it is rooted, this bouquet of cut flowers,
    In the feminine soul. But—and do not miss it—
a sailboat. Small, white, it floats just beyond:

the male force billowing and blossoming. Bouquet and boat,
    uniting opposites within the celestial light shining,
within the biggest flower's magical black eye.

Look into the eye of the flower, into the eye
    of God, the I of God. Bouquet and boat, flower and I,
real and unreal, male and female, all have become one.

Milton Avery's "Sea Grasses and Blue Sea"

The world is flat. Its colors uniform.
Its shapes geometric. Was nature ever more abstract?
More than abstract—inert. The opposite of Van Gogh's
"Starry Night," where even the sky roars like the sea.

Beneath that slender strip of unmoving sky,
the seascape is but two blue trapezoids—
the grasses, pale mirror of the sky,
the water, essence of all blue.

It is the waves one never forgets
(once shocked into recognizing them!)—
Avery's brave black waves in a blue blue sea.
For years I thought they were rocks,

ominous projections. Not so. Waves—
blacker than boulders, roughly rimmed,
flecked with only a suggestion of foam.
Blackcaps as far back as the eye can see!

Avery's black is the color of all light,
radiant as the whitest of whites.

Diane Arbus' Collaborations

I work from awkwardness. By that I mean
I don't like to arrange things. If I stand in
front of something, instead of arranging it,
I arrange myself. —D. A.

1. Russian Midget Friends in a Living
Room on 100th Street, N. Y. C., 1963

The couple sit close to one another,
their friend apart. She leans toward
them, hand on knee, show of slip below
cotton housedress. Their faces
are compact and wrinkled, overripe
autumn pears, the room dark as the floor's
linoleum. For a living room,
it is furnished oddly: chest of drawers,
dressing table, folding mirror elephantine
behind the Tom Thumb inhabitants.
The diminutive man sits in a Provincial
chair. On the dresser, a lamp shaped
like a bunny rabbit cheerfully stares.

2. The Junior Interstate Ballroom Dance
Champions, Yonkers, N. Y., 1962

They pose, suspended in perfect form,
she in waltz-length chiffon,
he in shawl-collar white dinner jacket.
They are not a day over fourteen.
Before them on the ballroom floor
rest twin gilt plastic trophies.
The piano is silent, the folding chairs
are empty, the dance floor is empty,
the stage is empty, but still they hold

their pose, their poise,
smiling emptily as the future.

3. *Mexican Dwarf in His Hotel Room in N. Y. C., 1970*

Propped in his rented bed, he confronts us
directly, mouth turned up
in opposition to his moustache.
His soft torso is naked, hairless
as a chihuahua. The towel which covers
his foreshortened lower half is grimy
—yet on his head perches a shapely hat!
To make him appear taller? A flair
for fashion? His toenails are pared.
His elbow rests upon a deal night stand
which holds his pint-sized whiskey
bottle, his pint-sized world.

4. *A Family on Their Lawn One Sunday in Westchester, New York, 1968*

Everything has been formalized. The normal couple
repose upon redwood chaise longues which match.
Between them a redwood table holds a drink,
a wallet, an ashtray, cigarettes. Behind them,
between picnic table and the swings,
their son bends over his plastic kiddie pool.
The trees which line their acres are evergreen.
She lies, eyes closed, hair unnaturally blonde,
face a replica of last decade's movie queen.
He lies with hand across his eyes, shielding
them from the sun, or pressed against
an oppressive hangover? What goes through
their minds? The lawn is thin.

5. Retired Man and His Wife at Home in a Nudist Camp One Morning, N. J., 1963

This is what he worked for all his life,
to sit surrounded by the paid-for possessions,
to relax and answer to no one. He regards the camera
unashamedly, wears only bedroom slippers,
his belly an appendage above his small penis.
His wife sits across the room wearing only sandals,
breasts lolling like eggplants, hands folded
between her legs. On the television her photo,
nude, younger, more slender days.
On the wall above his chair, a painting
of some idealized pinup—Marilyn Monroe
breasts, Betty Grable legs. The human body
is not all that it has been cracked up to be.

6. A Young Brooklyn Family Going for a Sunday Outing, N. Y. C., 1966

The wife is a beauty, eyebrows and hair
deliberately styled like Elizabeth Taylor's.
She holds a camera, a big pocketbook,
an imitation leopardskin coat, and an infant.
But the forlorn expression! Beside her poses
her husband, more casually attired: pullover,
short zip jacket, unbelted trousers.
His face is good-looking but defeated.
His right hand clasps their young son's,
who clasps his little groin and grins, retarded.

7. *Boy with a Straw Hat Waiting to March in a Pro-War Parade, N.Y.C., 1967*

The hat is a boater, the tie is a bow,
white shirt, V-neck sweater, dark suit.
He is the boy next door. On his lapel
he wears one pin and two buttons—
an American flag, a "God Bless America
Support Our Boys in Viet Nam,"
and a "Bomb Hanoi." In his right hand
another American flag.
Behind him a stone building looms,
solid as a bank, or an armory.

8. *Xmas Tree in a Living Room in Levittown, L.I., 1963*

The fringed bouclé sofa and polyester
wall-to-wall are immaculate. The lampshade
retains its cellophane. The star-burst
wallclock reads twenty minutes to one.
Early afternoon. This room is underfurnished:
sofa, carpet, blonde television, coffee table,
and one Christmas tree, trimmed with glass
balls, dripping tinsel. It looks like Sophie Tucker.
Beneath it repose a dozen presents,
richly wrapped. Compensation for the year's
deprivations? To stand it in this low room,
the top of the tree is severely lopped.
Never has a room appeared more lonely.

9. A Jewish Giant at Home with His Parents
in the Bronx, N. Y., 1970

They are conversing, but what has he to say
to them, or they to him? He cannot stand
in their house without stooping.
His mother looks up where his head looms
like the giant in Jack and the Beanstalk.
His father stands business-suited, white pocket
handkerchief. How did this proper couple
spawn a giant? He needs special orthopedic
shoes, leans upon a cane. All they ever asked for
was a nice son to take over the family business,
marry a nice Jewish girl. All they ever wanted
was to be proud. He makes them feel small.

10. Two Men Dancing at a Drag Ball,
N. Y. C., 1970

The face of the one who leads is turned away.
His shirt, suit and haircut would be at home
on Wall Street or Mad Ave. The face of his
partner is uplifted—defiant? Proud?
Or resigned to a life which has meaning
only after five o'clock when he can leave
the office, go home, don the gay apparel—
blonde wig, high heels, white gloves,
feathered gown downy as a baby egret.
Around the room they whirl, one manly,
one graceful as a little girl.

11. *Transvestite at Her Birthday Party,*
N.Y.C., 1969

The impossible hotel room on Broadway
and 100th Street has been decorated
with phallic-shaped balloons. A birthday
cake is centered on the bed. With Mona Lisa
hands folded, she reclines, bewigged,
wearing a short lace negligee, Fredericks
of Hollywood. She smiles, teeth reveal a gap
you could drive a truck through. The party
is the cake, one whore friend, her pimp,
and the photographer. The guests are nowhere
to be seen. The presents are nowhere.

12. *Masked Woman in a Wheelchair,*
Pa., 1970

Before a brick hospital or school
she is a figure reclining in a contraption
placed out-of-doors. Her useless legs
are blanket-wrapped. One hand clutches
a bag—for trick-or-treat goodies?
The other holds before her face a mask,
hideous and warty. She is the witch
on the watch for children, she is the crone
to whom Hansel and Gretel come.
She is the one whose body is all stove in.

13. *Young Couple on a Bench*
in Washington Square Park, N.Y.C., 1965

Two figures twine as one: his denimed thigh
swung across hers, her arm wrapped around
his bare back. They are a lyrical bas-relief
in the neoclassical style. Her expression,
dreamy; his, distracted. Tonight she will open
her thighs to him, his nipples will become
attentive eyes. Tonight they will toss
in the back seat of his third-hand Chevrolet.
Her mother worries. Paris takes Helen from Troy.

14. *Untitled (1), 1970-71*

Do they look this way because
they don't know any better,
or because they want to?
Two matrons, arms linked,
grin wide as jack-o'-lanterns,
wear outlandish flowered bonnets
tied with ribbons under the chin,
knee socks, shapeless cardigans.
Is it Hallowe'en, or are they
residents of an America where
every day is Hallowe'en? They face
the camera with uninhibited
delight. In the picture
-taking process, they collaborate.

V

The Wounded Angel

The Death of Janis Joplin

October 4, 1970

Oh, Lord, won't you buy me
a Mercedes-Benz! . . .

Because she was a white girl
    born black-and-blue,
because she was outsized victim
    of her own insides,
because she was voted
    "Ugliest Man on Campus,"
because she looked for something
    and found nothing—
    she became famous.

"Tell me that you love me!"
    she screamed at audiences.
They told. Fat Janis wouldn't
    believe. Twenty-seven,
a star since twenty-four,
    she tried to suck, lick,
smoke, shoot, drip, drop,
    drink the world.
    Nothing worked.

Bought a house, a place
    to go home to.
Bought a dog, something to give
    love to. Nothing worked.
Jimi Hendrix died, Janis cried:
    "Goddamn. He beat me
to it!" Not by much. Three weeks
    later she joined him.
    Part of something at last.

Letter from Nina

Please pardon the hand-written note
and try to send a copy to your brother.
I do not type and a long seige
of hot torrid humid weather
with very high pollution has put me
on the shelf. But not before

I had my birthday. Ninety years
seems like a mighty long time.
My friends do not believe it,
neither do I. Thanks for the flowers.
I always say, carnations last so.
Card from President and Nancy Reagan,

cards, letters, wires and phone calls
made me happy. I have a God-given talent,
playing the piano by ear. I was fortunate
to travel far and near, and have played
on many unique pianos: a mother of pearl
keyboard at "My Old Kentucky Home,"

Grieg's in his home on a Norwegian isle—
one of my many tours and excursions.
What became of the baby-grand VOSE piano
that graced your grandmother's parlor?
I always enjoyed playing it so.
She should have willed it to me.

Speaking of pianos, I have worn out four,
finally reached my goal—a STEINWAY!
I played "Maple Leaf Rag" at my party,
also performed a one-woman duet—
"Dixie" on the right hand, "Yankee Doodle"
on the left. One hundred guests and admirers.

(One made a fool of himself. He wore
a steel helmet with a burning candle
taped to the top, beat a bass drum
with HAPPY BIRTHDAY NINA painted on it.
Horace is seventy and has tried to get me
to marry him many times. Ha! No dice.)

I have played for and outlived all
the leading ballet teachers in this town.
I have played for ballroom dance classes
at Nashville Military Institute, fifty years.
I have been Supervisor of Culinary
at the Tennessee State Fair, fifty years.

My husband your great-uncle died in 1957.
A retired railroad man, as you know.
Once when he was younger all the boys
on the Louisville/Nashville line compared
their things. Honey, his was the longest.
And snapping black eyes all over his head.

After he died I took a business course
and had me a career for fifteen years.
I didn't retire until 1976 (lied
about my age). Now active in Senior Citizens
and Young-at-Heart Club. I write some.
I published a musical composition—

an old-fashioned two-step, real corny.
I had a daughter and a son, both deceased.
Seven grandchildren, thirteen great-grand,
three great-great, with—God help us—
one more on the way. What floors me,
not one of them has inherited my talent.

The New American Muse

is blonde and lives in California.
She doesn't look a day over twenty-two.

Her face is free of makeup,
her breasts have never known a bra.

She wears ripped jeans, her tee
shirt advocates *The Advocate*.

She doesn't drink much, but smokes
moderate amounts of grass.

She is into health foods,
jacuzzis, yoga, oral sex,

breakdancing, backpacking, EST.
Her vocabulary is astounding:

"Humungus," "airhead," "meganerd,"
"networking," "freebasing," "sleaze". . .

Frequently I see her hitchhiking
on the Freeway. No matter how

many times I stop and offer
a ride, she never gets in.

Heavenly Day for a Do:
A Pantoum

The Terrace. American Academy and
Institute of Arts and Letters. May.

"Heavenly day for a do!"
      "Here comes the Princeton contingent."
"They got Paul here—what a coup."
      "This punch tastes more like astringent."

"Here comes the Princeton contingent."
      "Mike Keeley and Joyce Carol Oates?"
"This punch tastes more like astringent."
      "That reporter's taking *notes*."

"Mike Keeley and Joyce Carol Oates?"
      "The proceedings were much too long."
"That reporter's taking notes."
      "He looks just like Anna May Wong."

"The proceedings were much too long."
      "Look: there's Buckminster Fuller."
"He looks just like Anna May Wong."
      "A shame about Henry Miller."

"Look, there's Buckminster Fuller!"
      "Isn't there anything to eat?"
"A shame about Henry Miller."
      "His acceptance speech was effete."

"Isn't there anything to *eat*?"
      "Helen's wearing a schmata."
"His acceptance speech was effete."
      "Vassar's his alma mater."

"Helen's wearing a schmata."
          "Oh, Norman's dyeing his hair!"
"Vassar's his alma mater."
          "Watch out for that snake Alastair."

"Oh, Norman's dyeing his hair!"
          "They got Paul here—what a coup."
"Watch out for that snake Alastair."
          "Heavenly day for a do."

More Things We Will Never Know

for, and after, Robert B. Shaw

What became of Delilah
your Dandie Dinmont terrier
who ran out to pee in the snow
and never returned

Or the slender jade garter
snake who wrinkled across
the living room carpet
one summer day, to disappear

Whatever happened to the black
lady in Grand Central Terminal
who never begged, but scratched
out a living with her voice

Who would have won the chess game
terminated by the president
of the World Chess Federation
after five months, 45 games

Is the Shroud of Turin for real
Where're Amelia Earhart and her plane
Did Jack the Ripper sit in Parliament,
Shakespeare pen all those plays

While we're at it, where in hell
is Howard Hughes' will? What are
the great Ed Sullivan-faced statues
on Easter Isle trying to say

How did the Pyramids get constructed
Was there ever an Atlantis, was JFK
Marilyn Monroe's lover, what made
your brother a religious fanatic

85

Why did they rip Pennsylvania Station
down? Was Anastasia daughter of the Czar
Was your wife still in love with G. A.
and just married you on the rebound

Were Hannibal's elephants Indian
or African? Would it matter
Would you have passed your orals
if you'd hung around a tad

Are the twins really yours
and whatever happened to Dagmar
and Jerry Lester? Why did they
fire-bomb Dresden, what makes

the Mona Lisa smile so
What was the iridescent mystery
meat they served every Sunday
in the university cafeteria

What will you never quite remember
from last night's deep dream
what was today's one perfect
unrecognized epiphany

when Grace descends will you
have the grace to know it
should you have bought an Edsel
as an investment? Why were you fired

Who have you turned away who could
have been the one most close
who if anyone will be by you
when they pull the plug?

Once Upon a Time

In Europe they lived like princess and prince,
not in a palace, though one graced the block,
and on Sundays they strolled in its gardens.
They gazed Narcissus-like into the pools,
their daughters chased mallards and rare black swans.

Their own house was a redone half-mansion
they couldn't hope to occupy in the States;
a winding staircase spun three stories high,
the windowpanes told bright, stained-glass fables,
the latticed gazebo in the back yard

bore roses which she watered every day
("*Jeden tag!*" their avuncular landlord
ordered, and she groaned but watered daily).
Participants in some vague fairy tale,
they walked the Rhine with the dressed-up Germans

and made wild love on their goose-feather bed.
Griffins and unicorns figured their dreams.
In two years they saw but two meager snows,
as those roses grew and their daughters grew,
and when they returned to America

she lost him, he lost her—Where did they go?

Chimney-Sweeper's Cry

Düsseldorf, 1972

Black my suit, black my top hat,
hands, face, black all black.
They stare as I pedal past
in a gang of sticks and brooms.
They tread the common stone.
I climb aloft cheerfully, descend
to sunless Hell: soot, char, old bat dung.

Ah, only the crookleg stork sings
more sweet than I! I am in
my element. There's a school
book proves man is most carbon.
It's in all that twitches!
Earth Mother's hands are pitch.
Fairer flowers spangle blackest soil.

'Twas the raven Noah first let go—
the raven, not the dove. Bah,
your white hero astride a white steed;
where are horse and hero now?
Lilies for a dead man's chest.
Black is lively, as here as now;
white? A faceless clock. Listen:

There is a northerly creature,
I know, the Abominable Snowman,
white raging in a whirl of white,
no blackguard's heart so vile as he.
I choose my broom, I lower myself.
Carbon alone becomes immortal diamond.
Alone through Hell Christ comes to shine.

The Balance

for Graham

Most boys learn to ride
two-wheel bikes with Father

at their side, pushing, holding,
encouraging, until the moment

Father drops back, unexpectedly,
and Boy—riding on his own—

spins out across the world.
But I was away on business

the birthday we gave you
your bike. Five-year-old,

you rolled it into the wide
European courtyard, parked

by the front steps, climbed,
mounted, pushed off, pedalled

into the gravelled drive,
fell, dragged it back, straddled

the saddle, fell and fell
and fell and fell again.

And when I returned home, after
dark, you were waiting there.

"Look! Look at me!" You biked
proud, erect, perfectly.

My balanced son, the world
that took you in was devoid of me.

Corn Flakes

That's all he knows
of food, or wants. Ten-year-old,
skin white as the milk
he pours into his bowl,
he and the flakes are flat,
a formica counter top,
scarcely dimensional.

Upstairs his mother is flat
on her back again. She passed
out sometime before his face
and teeth were scrubbed last night.
He filled the tub with tepid
tears. A hollow plastic
duck bobbed dumbly up and down.

That duck is broken in the head.
It lets the water in and drowns.
He watches it lurch, then sink.
Though it has lost its quack,
the boy won't let it go.
Together they've weathered
too many liquid nights of fear.

Whenever she doesn't tuck him in,
or scold him out of bed for school,
he rises and finds her on the floor.
Poor mommy. The box is easy to reach
and pour. They crackle. The shower
builds, sawdust in a bowl.
Last week I tried. I treated him

to steak, which he pushed aside.
"Corn flakes, please," he said.

Harlequin & Cock

for Tom Baker

Figure of night, bloodless Harlequin
identified by mask, fake motley,
is brilliant, but all but all buffoon.
At cock-crow he shrinks, hides, or like
some old Expressionist blinks at day—
cock of the night, no cock of the walk.

Cock, dawn-bird, sun-splendid in true
motley, decks the day out in feathers.
Like Matisse he stares unwinkingly
into the day's eye: Of course he bears
Priapus' name, ready. Unruined
as Cocteau, his song argues the first
glint, greets before the Resurrection
Christ, the world, his next recovery.

At the Summit

Milan Cathedral, 1972

for Evelyn Shrifte

A myriad carven statues
known only to the encircling air!
        At uncalculable points
        the profile of some little saint
gazes with bald marble eyes
onto vast indolent Lombardy,
        a pair of folded hands prays
        before bright, immediate Heaven,
sandalled feet planted
at the edge of the impossible abyss . . .

This whited world, lonely
as the snowfields of the higher Alps,
        sends with keen incision saintly limbs
        and spires to leap, to shoot,
assault the unsheltered blue,
their glow more glorious
        than that pitiless star,
        the Sun. Daily that orb staggers,
withdraws, dies—a wounded old general
within his tent of night.

But these sweet marble monks,
this youthful angelic population,
        unmelted, unintermittent,
        shines forever.

The Stigmata of the Unicorn

Musée de Cluny, 1975

for Vicky and Robert Pennoyer

Tapestry I

Two noblemen, two huntsmen,
    a bray of hounds, and a young prince
trouble the bluebells of Flanders.
    They stalk the miraculous. The tracker signals.
Just ahead the virtuous beast
    dips his purled horn into a stream.
The waters instantly purify.

Tapestry II

Goat's head, beard and feet,
    lion's tail and pride, the single
knurled horn—from his eye
    an unnatural blue light.
They ring him with their spears.
    He resists till he sees the decoy
virgin. Into their hands he commits
    his life. He falls upon his knees,
lays down his head upon her lap.
    They close in. They crucify.
Oh, the cry of the wounded unicorn!
    It shatters the bluebells.
It glitters in the air!

Tapestry III

Mortal wounds cannot slay.
    The cock crows, the unicorn rises
again, in glory, in a field fabulous with flowers.
    Stigmata glow on a field of snow.
His face spells forgiveness, hope, immortality.

The Wounded Angel

for Marlene Ekola Gerberick

It fell like a stone from the sky.
It lay in our potato field,
alien, injured, whimpering.
Kain and I dropped our hoes and ran

to see what it was cast down there.
At first all we could see were wings.
Then it—he!—sat up in a tuck.
One wing, broken, hung like a hinge.

When he saw us he dipped his head.
Downcast, his eyes soft as a hare's,
would not meet ours. We saw the blood
on his wonderful white garment.

What must an angel think, falling
through the dazzling air, stunned, surprised
to leave his brothers and sisters,
to land on this ponderous plot?

We tried to talk with him. Nothing.
Finally we decided to act.
We made a litter from bean poles,
carried him to town. He was light.

Not many saw us walking there,
it was the Sabbath—most slept or
were at church. (We'd broken the Word
to dig potatoes, Sunday morn.)

The few that saw us saw a sight:
two stocky boys in dark work clothes,
bearing an angel through the town!
His wings dripped feathers like white rain.

Where to, church father or doctor?
He seemed to be leaving this world.
We stopped before the doctor's stoop;
he took one look and was amazed.

He set to work on surgery,
stitched that wing with strong cat gut,
bathed and dressed the prodigious wounds,
indicated the need for rest.

We left the angel lying there,
on a cot in a dark back room
in a cottage roofed with green grass
in our tiny fishing village.

We returned to our fields, silent
with prayer that he would recover.
Dusk, we returned to the doctor's.
But the shy angel was not there.

The doctor said he'd locked the door
to make sure the patient was safe
from any who might come to pry.
Later, when he unlocked it—gone,

the cot and room unoccupied,
except one feather on the floor,
four feet long, angelically white.
There were no blood spots anywhere.

That was long ago. Kain is dead,
the doctor also. I'm infirm.
"It was some great white bird you saw,"
our wives and villagers chided.

Could that be what happened? Often
Kain and I returned to that field,
scanned the starfields above. Some nights
we stood in a snowstorm all white

as a great floating of feathers.
We felt them brush our face, our soul.
Did we see what we thought we saw?
We hoped to God it might be so.

VI

Survival Songs

The Stone Crab: A Love Poem

*Joe's serves approximately 1,000 pounds
of crab claws each day.*
—Florida Gold Coast Leisure Guide

Delicacy of warm Florida waters,
his body is undesirable. One giant claw
is his claim to fame, and we claim it,

more than once. Meat sweeter than lobster,
less dear than his life, when grown that claw
is lifted, broken off at the joint.

Mutilated, the crustacean is thrown back
into the water, back upon his own resources.
One of nature's rarities, he replaces

an entire appendage as you or I
grow a nail. (No one asks how he survives
that crabby sea with just one claw;

two-fisted menaces real as night
-mares, ten-tentacled nights cold
as fright.) In time he grows another—

large, meaty, magnificent as the first.
And one astonished day, *Snap!* It too
is twigged off, the cripple dropped

back into treachery. Unlike a twig,
it sprouts again. How many losses
can he endure? . . . Well,

his shell is hard, the sea is wide.
Something vital broken off, he doesn't
nurse the wound; develops something new.

The Demons & the Dance

The poet tap-dances on
a barrel, smiles without surcease.
He taps from dusk to dawn.
The poet tap-dances on
the lid, to hold the demons
down that press for their release.
The poet tap-dances on
a barrel, smiles without surcease.

Survivor's Song

All my good friends have gone away.
    The boisterous flight of stairs is bare.
There's nothing more I want to say.

First was Jean—she thought she was gay—
    drunk nightly on *vin ordinaire*.
All my good friends have gone away.

And where is Scotty B. today?
    So Southern, so doomed, so savoir-faire?
(There's nothing more I want to say.)

Sweet Hermione was third to stray.
    How her monologues smoked the air!
All my good friends have gone away.

Daniel, our beer-budget gourmet,
    no longer plays the millionaire.
There's nothing more I want to say

Except: My world's papier-mâché.
    I need them all—weren't they aware?
All my good friends have gone away.
There's nothing more I want to say.

"Affections Harden"

after a misprint in a poem
by Richard Howard

"Affectations" you must have meant,
    or rather, they were what Auden meant,
in the context out of which you quoted him.

But affections harden too, Richard:
    run a strict course more damaging
than mere affectation, which whether

of speech, or gesture, is a false assumption,
    the unnatural assumed—
behavioral aspiration which consumes.

Affection, by definition, is a feeling
    or emotion defined, a natural
impulse swaying the mind.

The former exhibits the unreal,
    the latter settles a good will
or zeal. Both lay hold. Hardening

can be strengthening: viz. vulcanization.
    Not so with me. I lose in love,
gain the leathery slap of the glove.

Once I had a teacher, who encouraged
    cleverness, till she thought I became
too . . . too what? It's hard to say.

Once I had a friend, huge-hearted,
    mirthful, a clown. Fame calcified
his features; they took a hard line.

And once I had a lover, who stood still,
    a yellow willow in the snow.
Like Daphne, she closed all limbs to me.

What happens to the heart, hard hit?
    Affection, pressed, turns affectation:
indurate, enduring, a shell against the rain.

The Persistence of Memory,
the Failure of Poetry

In 1979, a New York high school
music student, Renée Katz, was pushed
in the path of a subway train.

The severed hand flutters
    on the subway track,
like a moth. No—

it is what it is,
    a severed hand.
It knows what it is.

And all the king's doctors
    and all the king's surgeons
put hand and stump together

again. Fingers move,
    somewhat. Blood circulates,
somewhat. "A miracle!" reporters

report. But it will only
    scratch and claw, a mouse
behind the bedroom wall. We forget.

At four a.m. the hand
    remembers: intricate musical
fingerings, the metallic

feel of the silver flute.

The Caves of Childhood

The giant elms of memory are gone.
In their place, lonely stumps keep vigil,
Confederate generals quadruply amputated.

The railroad I used to walk, tracks
gleaming in the sun, a twin-barrelled
shotgun, is unspiked and yanked.

Grandfather's dirt farm has been modernized.
The outside pump which gurgled then gushed
sweetwater is past its prime. The farm

house, breezewayed, three-car garaged.
The one-room schoolhouse sells ceramics,
ashtrays, plaster of Paris yard gnomes.

Stones are rolling across the cave openings
of childhood. They grind into place,
block out all light. With other boys

I used to explore those cramp corridors,
one cavern shaped like the human heart.
A majority of mushrooms bristled the floors.

Overhead bats hung like hooded stalactites.
Garter snakes flicked like green lanyards
disappearing into rock. Who was afraid?

At the auction block the melons are yellowed,
little jaundiced mongoloid babies. In the city,
the assassin crouches and flashes his knife.

A Garden Sitter

for William Heyen

Escape from the adult
world to my private place
was easy those afternoons.
Summer deepened into summer.

I slipped outside and skipped
through the big back yard
to the little rough lawn chair
made of unskinned logs,

its bark shaggy as a yak.
It stood in the sun by a bed
of zinnias and marigolds—
an explosion of yellow and orange!

I sat in my little chair
and loved the liveliness
and wonder—flowers, bees,
ants, grass, birds . . .

Bunch beans trembled behind,
the future yawned before.
I breathed deep and the green
from boxwood entered my lungs.

Islanded by half a life's time
and miles from those after-
noons, I sit quietly in a chair
and attempt to recapture surprise.

Transfer of Title

It's mine now. I mash
the accelerator and the Buick
monsters up my expensive hill,

its 1959 dorsal fins
thoroughly outrageous now.
It's a fish out of water.

But new, this Buick looked razzy
as some henna-haired hussy, the mistress
you never had. Dirt-farmer,

dirt-poor, you cashed all your insurance
for it. Mother and Father
thought you'd gone mad.

Grandfather, your last fling
transports me through a world
I'm making, a world you never knew:

A neighborhood where color TVs
flicker sickly through every picture-
window, where Thunderbirds

come to roost in every drive.
It's quite the oldest thing
in sight, steel and chromium

symbol of my relative
poverty. But I need it.
Its padded dash is a bosom

to comfort me if I fall.
Its directional signals
wink confidence for me.

This Buick's body is heavy as love.
Who would ever have thought
it would outdrag you?

You, who hoed one hundred rows,
then crowbarred the tin roof
off the garage all in one day?

It still burns hardly any oil,
while you lie hospitalized, anesthetized,
your points and plugs shot to hell.

Old People

In late afternoon they come out to think
on screened-in porches and breezeways.
They have billfolds with cracked yellow plastic
photo compartments, pass the protected
pictures around: son in school cap and gown,
daughter in gossamer bridal gown.
None of son with potbelly extended,
none of daughter with missing lower plate.

In late afternoon they come out to drink
on screened-in porches and breezeways.
When we come in they remind us we've grown
bald, have assumed countenances of great
grandparents. They say we don't remember,
they remember, when we were sucking tit.
By early evening they have become drunk
on memory. We take them home, tuck them in.

Tree Sequence

1

In Delaware the sassafras,
aromatic as rootbeer
or Mother's tea, cast silhouettes
upon my night ceiling.
Sleepless, I watched the dumb show
of trimorphous leaves—
some oval, some mitten-shaped,
some with three fat fingers—
jerk like shadow puppets.
Cats, dogs, sheep, goats,
a friendly menagerie.

2

In New York the ailanthus
in the private courtyard
tapped upon our glass.
Favorite food of silkworms,
tree of the gods, good omen,
companion, reality, it bore
great shade and mythology.
We set our newly married roots
into city cement. Manhattan
was the center of the universe.
There was nothing we would not try.

3

In Düsseldorf the linden,
German lime-tree, lifted limbs
to cathedral the park paths.
The heart-shaped leaves
and flowers of cream and gold
clusters, fairytaled us away.
What deep shadows, what mystery!

Angels and birds in its foliage,
lions, stags, unicorns under its shelter.
A pink palace beckoned beyond.
We would live forever.

4

In Westchester County the red pines—
that deep forest which rings
the reservoir like Druids,
descendants of enchanted Attis,
dropping shiny needles to the floor,
dropping woody cones to the floor,
making a Norway of the suburbs—
that circle of soothsayers is dead.
A rust or blister ran through faster
than fire. Driving by, haggard and balding,
I avoid the skeletons against the sky.

5

In my dreams the arbor vitae
rustles labyrinthine leaves.
Invariably it appears to me
upside down, its great roots
in heaven, its umbrella on earth.
A downward inclination, like life,
its shadow makes me euphoric.
That tree of trees is entirely laved
in the warm light of the sun.
It links the different worlds
of me. It is the ladder I descend.

6

In Delaware the cypress
survive crown gall, stem canker,
root rot, to prevail in Trussem Pond.
Northernmost stand on the continent,

they reach eighty feet aloft,
rise thin from fat pyramid trunks,
Giacomettis in hipboots. They watch
over bass and pickerel fishermen,
highways which pass for progress.
I return to beginnings: air
and water, earth and trees.

Miss Crustacean

for Cynthia Macdonald

I

"All my life I've wanted to be
Miss Crustacean!" I said into
the microphone, into the TV
cameras just after they crowned me
beauty queen at the Crab Derby.
Afterward my brother told me
what a fool I'd made of myself—

It was the first year they'd held
a beauty pageant at the Derby:
How could I have coveted the title
"all my life"? I know, I know.
But all my eighteen years ached
for recognition, some way.
All my eighteen years ached.

I always had blue limbs. In high
school I bumped into every open
locker door, my upper arms and thighs
blue with bruises, clumsiness.
In the class play I tripped

on my train, forgot my lines . . .
Not everything turned out badly:

I was a good swimmer. My best stroke,
the crawl. I struggled with one poem—
about nature being "red in tooth
and claw." I longed for
Donald Lee Scruggs to ask me
to the Junior-Senior Prom.
Donald Lee was a swimmer.

When he didn't ask me, I asked him.
Only to be told he was taking
Sue-Ellen Wheatley, captain
of the girls' basketball team.
She never bumped into anything.
Fortunately, the Crab Derby
was held on Labor Day Weekend,

I hadn't been near a locker
for three months! Not one bruise.
I possessed a certain beauty.
I was confident. And that day,
a gorgeous early September day
in Crisfield, Maryland,
I became: Miss Crustacean.

II

In the year of my reign I took
my role seriously: rode through
parades in open convertibles,
attended banquets, promoted
crab meat best I could.
The following Labor Day
I returned to Crisfield to crown
my successor (Sue-Ellen Wheatley).

When I sidled up to the throne
to place my crown upon her head,
I realized I'd walked crabwise.
That was the beginning. In the years
to follow, I caught myself scuttling
about town, nails decorated
with orange-red gloss, arms bruised
cerulean blue. *Scuttle, scuttle*.

(I still lived at home, an old maid.
It was my own bureau drawers bruised
me blue now.) Every day I went
to swim in the unnatural blue waters
of the YWCA. In the warm element
I waved my claws in and out.
I wanted to swim nude, my pure
white abdomen lustrous alabaster.

But the Y requires tank suits.
I tread water. I acquire faster open
-water speed, dive to the bottom
to bury myself. For hours
I practice my crawl. Afterward,
in direct sunlight, I blink,
my stalked eyes, nubby horns.

How I hate direct sunlight!
After swimming, famine. My life
is swimming and one constant search
for food. At the Blue Dolphin Diner
they tease about how much I eat.
Anything in a pinch. I burn
it off. My parents worry:
They say my disposition has become

. . . crabby. If only they knew!
I need a new hobby, they say.
I considered shadowboxing.

Before the mirror at night
I stand in my room, slowly jabbing
the air with my powerful right
claw. I wave it like a flag.
Jab, jab, jab.

III

The preceding pages were written
(in my crabbed hand) some years ago.
They represent a reasonable account
of my existence for twenty years.
Today my swimming has slowed,

but my love of water never ceases.
My body, shell-white from every day
inside that sunless pool. I have lost
all interest in mating. My attitude
has hardened. I am more vague;

"She believes in the oblique,
indirect method," I heard someone say.
True. My walk, slower too. Yet
that supports my illusions—walking
legs slightly doubled, ready to spring!

But suddenly my life has changed.
First I feared cancer. That seemed
predetermined, the crab's pincers biting
my guts like hell. Now I know it is
something even more insidious. Everything

about me, even my brain, is . . . softening.
I lie in a darkened room in my bed
for days. I feel it at my points,
I feel it in my joints. Any moment now,
my entire shell will crack and bust.

VII
Body Icons

The Skin Game

Oh to be an onion!
Wonderful translucent
integuments, endless layers
of derma and epidermis,
membrane upon membrane
encircling the secret core!
Search for the heart of the onion
and find still another skin.
Search for the heart of the onion
and find yourself, crying.
The onion never cries.

I am no onion. My skin
so thin, stenographers
type memoranda on it.
Politicians draw treaties
upon it, barbarians shear it,
wear it about hairy shanks.
Enemies use it to make lampshades
(and call that my shining hour).
Hunters track me across the ice
like Little Eva, and flay me,
still alive . . .

Last week I bought a wet suit.
I wear it all the time.
I clop down the street in it,
flop down into bed in it.
Tough, rubbery, resilient,
it's like zipping myself inside
a deboned black man's hide.
It's being Huckleberry Finn
inside strong Nigger Jim.
It's not as many skins as the onion,
but it is one more.

Vital Message

The last thing I put on
    every morning is my

heart. I strap it to my
    wrist sheepishly, a man

with expensive friends
    exposing his Ingersoll.

But I strap it.
    Outside my sleeve it ticks

away the Mickey Mouse
    of my days. Some people

pretend not to notice. They look
    everywhere else but.

Some people touch it
    to see if it's warm.

It is. Warm as a hamster.
    One open-hearted friend

tried to give me
    a transplant. It wouldn't take.

I was left with my old,
    bleeding. A critic tried

to boil it in acid. It shrunk
    smaller than a chicken's.

One girl broke it. It crunched
    open, a Chinese cookie.

No fortune inside. One girl
    won it. She pats it,

a regular Raggedy Andy. And its
    worst enemy is me. I want

to eat it. Nail chewers know
    how tempting!—a plump purple

plum just above the wrist.
    It bursts with a juicy sigh.

The skin shreds sweet. No seeds.
    So far I only nibble the edges.

There is more than half left.

The Head

Somewhere between your house
      and my house
I lost my head.

Not Walter Raleigh style,
      but gently—a child's
balloon suffused

with helium,
      adrift on the spring air
a surprised afternoon.

It floated over willows
      washing their hair
in silver pools,

sailed above clouds
      pale as cow's milk.
It drifted toward the city

over steeples and aerials
      prickly as a populous
pincushion. It survived,

and came to rest
      outside your fourteenth-
floor window. It hung

around all day,
      a faithful dog
wanting in.

It peered through
      the dusty glass,
a prurient window-washer.

You were there.
        You never looked up
from your writing

desk. It wondered if
        you didn't care,
or if, miraculously,

you never once
        saw beyond the paper
sea to the blue beyond?

A head has no hands
        to knock with. So
it bunted,

a baby socking it
        to you in the womb.
No response.

At dusk it shrugged
        a neckless shrug,
mooned around the sill,

nuzzled the cool pane,
        a fish lipping
an aquarium tank.

Dank with dew,
        it shivered and dozed.
The sun rose, full of itself,

the head began
        to dwindle. Soon it hung
limp as a spent cock,

without the satisfaction.
A banner in defeat, it sagged,
fell to the sidewalk

with a slight thud.
No one picked it up.
Wrinkled, shapeless thing!

Unsightly as a bladder,
unwanted as a used condom,
children kicked it around

like a dead cat. Dogs shat on it.
Women dug stiletto heels
into it. Fourteen floors

above it all, you
ran snow-veined hands
through fiery hair,

selected a virgin
sheaf of paper, dipped pen
in ice, and wrote.

Hand Poem

My hand is my face.
—Edith Sitwell

My hand shaved me
    before work each day,

saved me in church
    high Holy Days,

punched me in
    before work days,

punched out enemies
    after work days,

earned me overtime
    hungry days,

picked my guitar
    in town Saturdays,

rowed me 'cross lakes
    crazy summer days,

pleasured me
    lonely winter days—

I was only a hired
    hand, sometimes a helping

hand, but always a happy
    hand, till I gave

my hand in marriage.
    She grabbed it,

kissed it, powdered it,
    wrapped it in pink

tissue paper, sealed
    it in Saks Fifth Avenue

cardboard, abandoned it
    to turn blue and die

deep in her vanity.

The Tenant

First you carefully slit
my throat from ear to ear
and pulled the flap way back,
an entrance to the wigwam

of my chest, made semi-
circular incisions beneath
my armpits, then carved clean
down each side. Foot braced

against my pelvis, you ripped
the whole flap down, skinning
this cat from chin to belly.
I was open, an unzipped sleeping bag.

You crawled inside, drew the flap.
It sealed tight and final
as Hansel and Gretel's oven.
Now your games begin:

You tap tap tap on my tired brain
with a little lead hammer
like an aspirin commercial,
my bones clang and bang—

ice-cold plumbing attacked
by some irate tenant.
You voodoo hat pins
into my doll-like heart,

kick against my belly: Feel
the world's largest foetus! See
the world's first pregnant man!
Every bite I eat nourishes you,

you funnel off every drink.
When I fast, you suck my blood.
Already I've dropped forty pounds.
When I sleep, you project old horror

movies in the theater of my skull.
When I wake, you make my eyes mist,
spraying Windex on the mirrors
of my soul. I grind, blind Samson,

while you, a sailor, haul anchor,
pull my guts. You've an open-
ended lease, free heat and water,
the garbage is collected regularly—

I'll never get rid of you.

The Pregnant Man

Alone and at 3
AM felt the first
twinge but thought
it something I ate
(cucumbers especially
big ones do that,
also radishes), but
at 4 AM the waters
broke, ran for a towel
to sponge the sheets
(what would my wife
say?), at 5 AM
the rhythms started
regular as Lawrence Welk,

at 6 AM called
my doctor, but he didn't
believe me, called my friends'
answering services, but
they didn't believe. At 6:30
called a taxi but it
didn't, and at 8
on the button, open
as a bellows, clutching
the bedpost, screaming
between gold inlays,
a duck squeezing out
a Macy's Thanksgiving
parade balloon, gave birth
to an eight-pound blue
-eyed bouncing baby
poem. Spanked it to life,
lay back and had a drink.

P.S.
Two hours later

131

it died. You know
how it is with poems.
(My last one had two
heads and no heart.)

The Invisible Man

No one looks up
when I come into a room.
Someone sits down on me
when I occupy a chair.
People stretch on top of me
when I lie in bed.
I am an invisible man.
My words, empty cartoon balloons.

My motives, totally transparent.
But there are advantages.
I don't worry about a wardrobe.
When people don't know you're there,
it doesn't matter which suit
you wear. Sometimes I like
being an invisible man.
I can eavesdrop on all,

observe all idiosyncrasies.
Last night I hunkered beside
your bed, smoked cigarettes
while you and your lover humped.
I blew smoke rings in his face.
He thought he was catching cold.
But mostly I hate invisibility.
It's being alone on a desert isle,

waving a raggy flag at airplanes
that pass and never land.
Of course, you could help.
You could acknowledge my presence,
come at me with your crayon set.

Look: Scribble in my hair, my eyes,
my mouth, limb my body's tree.
Give some color to my life.
I'm a person! (That too is a dream.)

The Empty Man

A cup before coffee, a shell
      after the scrambled egg,
I am a big nothing
      inside. A hole. A hideous
gaping vacuole. X-rayed, I
      reveal a TV set
after the repairman removes the tube.
      Nothing turns me on.

I tried to fill myself
      with hope. It sprang
eternal, for a little while. But
      there is no future in it.
I tried to fill myself
      with history. But the past
is undeveloped, a thin black film.
      Nostalgia is not what it used to be.

I tried to cram myself
      with literature. I became
a stuffed owl: Dickinson and Dickens.
      Diderot and Sappho, Colette
and Kant, Shakespeare and Etcetera.
      In the end,
they proved indigestible.
      In the end, they turned to shit.

I tried to fill myself with you.
      I funneled all your brunette hair,
brown-eyedness, energy, optimism
      and tits. All inside.
I poured you on. But my ass
      had a hole in it. You leaked
away. Your beautiful essence drained
      like dirty bath water.

I tried to siphon off my best friend.
    His liver, his lights,
his action, his camera. I identified.
    I stole his walk, talk, wink,
stink. I sucked him through a straw.
    I, Dracula, succubus, lived
off him for months. The faster I absorbed,
    the slower I spun:

A running-down top,
    a drunken dervish whirl,
going everywhere, getting nowhere,
    my life staggered to a stop.
A decapitated chicken, it fell
    on its side. Help! I'm a key
-hole without a key. Help! I'm an eye
    without a hook. Can *you* satisfy?

The Silent Man

Speech is dirty silence.
—Wallace Stevens

Silence is not golden.
Is whitest white—
an untrampled snowfield.

Not silence of the grave:
peace before a storm.
Hush before utterance.

Silence of possibility.
Taciturn, I preserve
stillness. Soundlessness.

Try. I invite you. Seal
your lips. Hold your breath.
Keep unruffled the white

velvet cloak of silence.
Some people will say,
He was struck dumb! No,

there simply is nothing
to say worth breaking
this white silken web.

The Tough Man

*The Numidians burn the scalps of their
infant children with coals, to make them
less sensitive to the action of the sun,
which is so fierce in their country.*
                                        —after Herodotus

I should have been raised a Numidian.
To skirmish through life unfeeling, unfelt.
The sun himself could not get me fired up
(not to mention certain *saftig* girls
seen in the streets, or lovers I have met
and meet and meet and repeat . . .).

How much safer if I had been calloused
thick as an old rhinoceros' hide!
When I poked myself, I'd surely not feel
superior—my heart is soft as yours.
It is, quite simply, a way to survive.
Make the fire brighter. Now bring me my son.

The Married Man

I was cut in two.
Two halves separated
cleanly between the eyes.
Half a nose and mouth on one
side, ditto on the other.
The split opened my chest
like a chrysalis, a part
neat in the hair.
Some guillotine slammed
through skull, neck, cage,
spine, pelvis, behind—
like a butcher splits
a chicken breast.

    I never knew which side my heart
    was on. Half of me sat happy
    in a chair, stared at the other
    lying sad on the floor. Half wanted
    to live in clover, half to breathe
    the city air. One longed to live
    Onassis-like, one aspired to poverty.
    The split was red and raw.

I waited for someone to unite me.
My mother couldn't do it. She claimed
the sissy side and dressed it like a doll.
My father couldn't do it. He glared
at both sides and didn't see a one.
My teachers couldn't do it. They stuck
a gold star on one forehead,
dunce-capped the other.

    So the two halves lived in a funny house,
    glared at one another through the seasons;
    one crowed obscenities past midnight,
    the other sat still, empty as a cup.

One's eye roadmapped red from tears,
the other's, clear and water-bright.
Stupid halves of me! They couldn't even
decide between meat and fish on Fridays.
Then one began to die. It turned gray as old meat.

Until you entered the room
of my life. You took the hand of one
and the hand of the other
and clasped them in the hands of you.
The two of me and the one of you
joined hands and danced about the room,
and you said, "You've *got* to pull yourself
together," and I did, and we are two
-stepping our lives together still,

    and it is only when I study hard
    the looking glass I see that one
    eye is slightly high, one corner
    of my mouth twitches—a fish on a hook—
    whenever you abandon me.

The Cultivated Man

I came from dust and must return,
but in between was living a dust-life, too.
That seemed anything but fair,
dry roots stunted in a walking dustheap.

Even my sister, the moon, was not so barren,
her surface not so bald. My eyes? Instruments
recording thirty-five years' drought. My heart,
a forgotten avocado seed. Then you flew

over the field of my life, an emergency helicopter
dropping your little CARE packages. I looked up,
saw you at the controls, brimming with more
fruits and vegetables than Carmen Miranda's hat.

I felt the twitch of the seed within the center
of the pod. I knew the industry of the beetle
pushing its dung ball. I tell you, the sun danced
over a mountain that day! The sun wore silver boots.

And that is when I vowed to farm
myself. To clear away the winter stubble.
There were truckloads of husk and tangle.
It was weeks before I saw my way clear.

Then I harnessed myself to my own plow
and broke the ground. Each heave a beginning.
The neighbors came to watch, cleave together,
a cop had to come direct traffic.

Someone sold pop corn, soda pop, even programs.
"He's no farmer," the multitude agreed. I didn't care.
All that was beside the point. The point was,
I was a lout and had to cultivate myself.

I waited for the right time of month,
I waited for the moon to put on her best face.
When soil was ready and moon was ready
and I was ready, I fertilized with a fish.

I dressed that ground like a bride.
I sowed all my seeds. Some fruits, some vegetables,
but some notions of my own, too:
little red maples, because they are liveliest,

poppies because they make the most seeds.
And now I sit and wait for rain and for you
to slip away from your yellow kitchen.
Come, we can dance in the furrows. Come, we can hop

like two rain toads. Hop is a word like hope,
only more immediate. I can milk the cow whose udder
is the moon, I can skin the hare that haunts
the moon. After this, I can do anything.

ABOUT THE AUTHOR

ROBERT PHILLIPS has published three previous books of poetry: *Inner Weather* (1966), *The Pregnant Man* (1978), and *Running on Empty* (1981). Individual poems of his have appeared in *The American Poetry Review*, *The Hudson Review*, *The New Yorker*, *The Paris Review*, *The Partisan Review*, *Poetry*, and many other journals, as well as the *Pushcart Prize* anthology.

A respected fiction writer, critic, editor, and reviewer as well, Phillips has most recently brought out *The Collected Stories of Noël Coward*, *Letters of Delmore Schwartz*, and *The Stories of Denton Welch*. His reviews have appeared in *Commonweal*, *The New York Times Book Review*, *Saturday Review*, and other periodicals.

Born in Delaware in 1938, Phillips now lives in Katonah, New York, where he has directed the poetry reading series at the Katonah Village Library for the past eighteen years.

ONTARIO REVIEW PRESS POETRY SERIES